GO FACTS ANIMALS
Insects

A & C BLACK • LONDON

Insects

contents

© Blake Publishing Pty Ltd 2002
Additional Material © A & C Black Publishers Ltd 2003

First published 2002 in Australia by Blake Education Pty Ltd

This edition published 2003 in the United Kingdom by
A&C Black Publishers Ltd, 37 Soho Square, London W1D 3QZ
www.acblack.com

ISBN 0-7136-6590-4

A CIP record for this book is available from the British Library.

Written by Katy Pike
Science Consultant: Dr Max Moulds, Entomologist, Australian Museum
Design and layout by The Modern Art Production Group
Photos by Photodisc, Stockbyte, John Foxx, Corbis, Imagin, Artville and
Corel

UK Series Consultant: Julie Garnett

Printed in Hong Kong by Wing King Tong Co Ltd

A & C Black uses paper produced with elemental chlorine-free pulp,
harvested from managed sustainable forests.

What is an Insect?

Insects are small animals with six legs and three body parts.

Insects have three main body parts. These three parts are the **head**, the **thorax** and the **abdomen**.

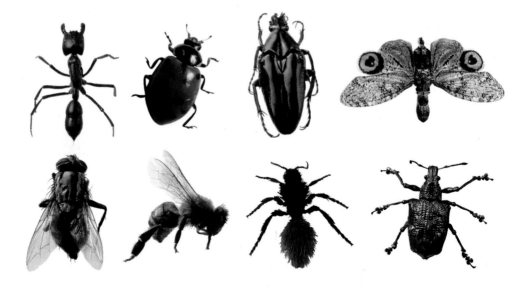

All insects have two **antennae**. They use their antennae for touch, taste and smell.

Insects do not have bones. They have a hard shell that protects their bodies. This hard shell is called an **exoskeleton**.

4

Some grasshoppers
can fly.

 # Types of Insects

The insect world has a large number of species. There are more than 800 000 types of insects.

Many insects have wings. Insects fly to collect food and to escape from danger. Butterflies, beetles and bees can fly.

Some insects live together in large groups called **colonies**. Ants, bees and wasps live in colonies.

Insects feed in two ways. Some insects bite and chew their food. Ants and caterpillars feed this way. Others suck their food up through a hollow tube. Butterflies, mosquitoes and flies feed this way.

A honeybee's wings beat
200 times per second.

A dragonfly can
fly very fast.

Wasps chew
their food, such
as this plum.

7

Butterflies are insects with big wings. They have six legs and three main body parts.

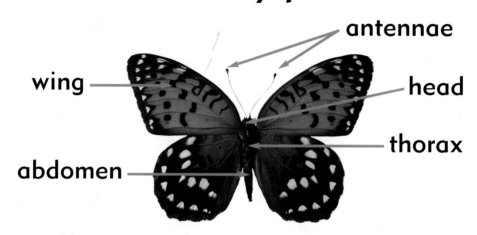

The three main body parts of a butterfly are the head, the thorax and the abdomen. A butterfly also has wings. It uses its colourful wings to fly and to attract mates.

A butterfly has two antennae. It uses them to touch, taste and smell.

All butterflies begin life as caterpillars. The caterpillars change into butterflies. This change is called **metamorphosis**.

A birdwing butterfly gets ready to fly.

GO FACTS

BIGGEST!

The wingspan of a birdwing butterfly is as big as an adult's pair of hands.

Insect	Number of species
butterflies	15 000
moths	120 000

Life Cycle of a Butterfly

How a butterfly grows from an egg to an adult.

1 Butterflies lay their eggs on a plant. Each egg hatches into a caterpillar.

2 The caterpillar eats some of the plant and grows quickly.

3 The caterpillar covers itself in a hard shell called a **chrysalis**. Inside the chrysalis, its body changes.

4 The butterfly breaks out of the chrysalis.

egg

butterfly

caterpillar

chrysalis

Bees

Bees are flying insects. They have six legs and three main body parts.

wing — head

abdomen — antenna

thorax —

leg

A bee has a head, a thorax and an abdomen. A bee also has two pairs of wings. It has two antennae that it uses to touch, taste and smell.

Honeybees live in large colonies called **hives**. Bees live and work in the hive. Every hive has one queen bee. Some bees look after the queen bee and the young, growing bees.

Other bees fly out of the hive to look for food. They collect **nectar** and pollen from flowers.

These honeybees are working in the hive.

DID YOU KNOW?

The queen bee can lay up to 1500 eggs a day.

Insect	Number of species
honeybees	1 000
wasps	110 000

Life Cycle of a Bee

How a honeybee grows from an egg to an adult.

1 The queen bee lays all the eggs. She lays each egg inside a **honeycomb** cell.

2 Each egg grows into a **larva**. Worker bees feed and care for the larva.

3 The larva grows into a **pupa**. The pupa changes into a bee.

4 The adult bee breaks out of the honeycomb. Growing from egg to adult takes about three weeks.

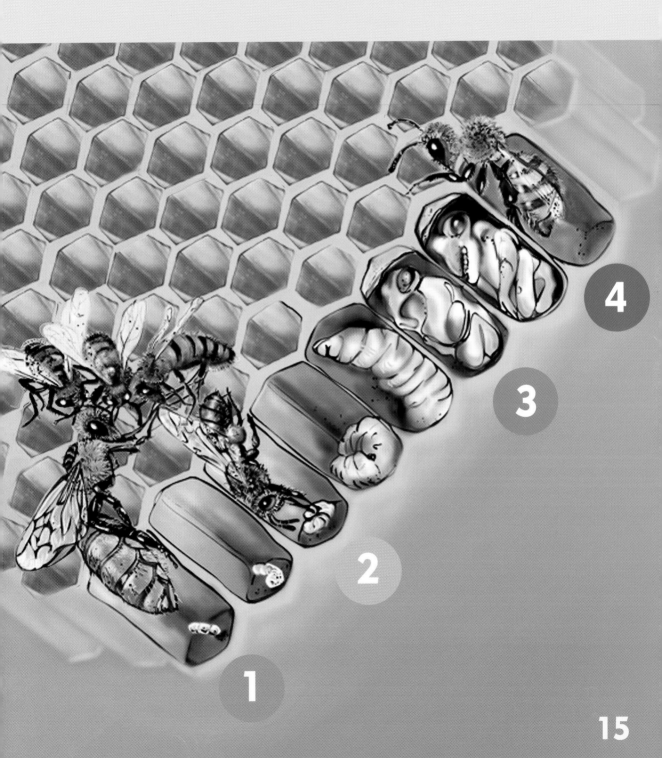

Ants

Ants are insects. They have six legs and three main body parts.

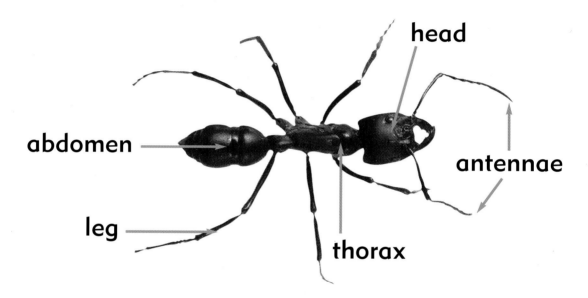

head

abdomen

antennae

leg

thorax

An ant has three main body parts. These three parts are the head, the thorax and the abdomen.

An ant has two antennae. It uses them to touch, taste and smell.

Ants live in large colonies called nests. A nest has many rooms.

These ants are carrying eggs and larvae.

DID YOU KNOW?

Leaf-cutter ants are farmers. They carry leaves back to their nest, chew them up and grow a fungus on them. All the ants in the nest eat the fungus.

Insect	Number of species
ants	over 8 000

Life Cycle of an Ant

How an ant grows from an egg to an adult.

1 Every ant colony has a queen ant who lays all the eggs. Worker ants carry the eggs to other rooms in the nest.

2 A larva hatches out of each egg. Nurse ants feed and care for the larvae.

3 Each larva covers itself in a firm shell. It is now called a pupa.

4 After two or three weeks, the adult ants break out of their shells.

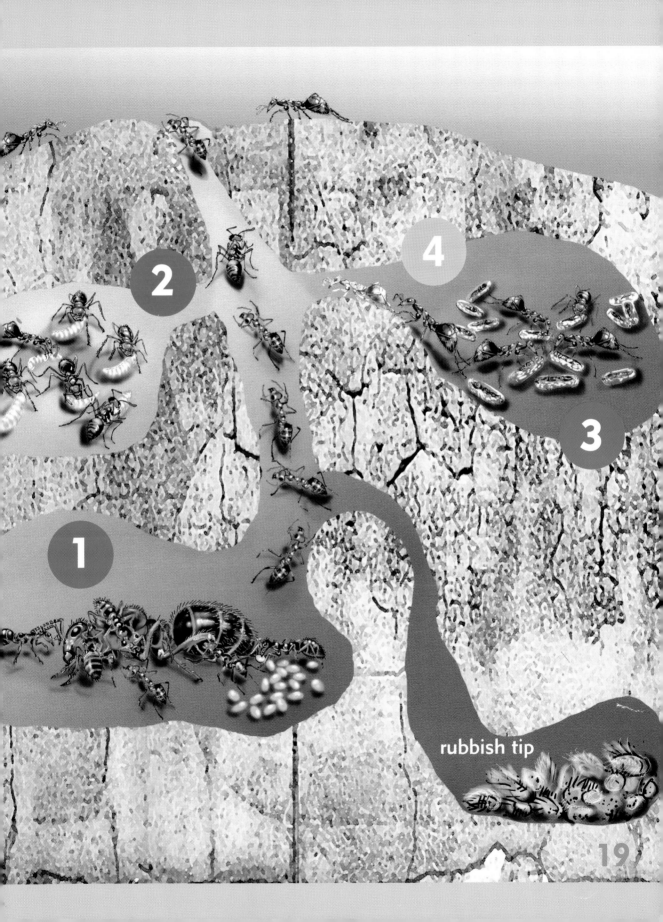

rubbish tip

19

Beetles

Beetles are insects. They have six legs and three main body parts.

head

antennae

thorax

abdomen

leg

The three main body parts of a beetle are the head, the thorax and the abdomen.

One pair of wings is hidden under hard outer wings. These outer wings form a hard shell over the beetle's body.

There are many different types of beetles. There are more beetles than any other insect. They live all over Earth, except in the oceans.

You can see two pairs of wings on this ladybird beetle.

How Do Insects Grow?

	1	2	3	4
butterfly	egg	caterpillar	pupa	adult
ant	egg	larva	pupa	adult
bee	egg	larva	pupa	adult
beetle	egg	grub	pupa	adult

22

Glossary

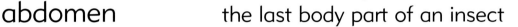

abdomen	the last body part of an insect
antennae	the feelers on an insect's head for touch, taste and smell – one feeler is called an antenna
chrysalis	the shell around a pupa
colony	a group of animals living together
exoskeleton	the skeleton on the outside of an insect's body
hive	a home for honeybees
honeycomb	wax rooms in a beehive
larva	a soft, wormlike, young insect – the plural is larvae
metamorphosis	the change from one form to another
nectar	a sweet food from plants that bees make into honey
pupa	the insect inside a chrysalis – the plural is pupae
thorax	the insect body part between the head and the abdomen

Index